Praise for
Celebrating Christmas

'Amy captures the true spirit of Christmas in this book that touches the heart and lifts the soul. Daughter and father, wordsmith and artist, combine seamlessly to create a celebration of the warmth, love, promise and glory of Christ's birth on earth, and what that means for us today.'
Pam Rhodes, broadcaster and writer

'In this love-filled book, created across the generations of a family, a father's paintings and his daughter's skilled writing offer us new perspectives on the meaning of Christmas. The combination of wise words with beautiful images weaves the joy and nostalgia of the festive season together with the deep truths of the story we celebrate. This will be a book that comes out with the decorations and the tree every year and quickly becomes a part of the season.'
Amy Scott Robinson, author of *Image of the Invisible*

'Like the chef of some ultimate Christmas pudding, how wonderfully Amy gently blends her choice ingredients: reflections on the Bible, memories of Christmases white, blue and granite grey – joyous and lonely – candlelit services, divine encounter, and family practices, all offered to us to taste and see if they might bring us closer to him who came to draw us close. Here then, in word and skilful paint, is not just an invitation to think about Christmas differently, but a winsome invitation to live it differently, more attentively, in turn drawing us on not just to see Christmas afresh but to see life afresh – Immanuel, Christ with us.'

Mark Greene, author of *Adventure: Christmas poems*

'*Celebrating Christmas* is like opening a box of your favourite chocolates. You think you know what you're going to get, only to discover a delightful surprise with each bite. Amy's collaboration with her father Leo adds a further layer of joy on this short journey of celebrating Immanuel, "God with us". The blending of inspirational thought with touching personal anecdotes and beautiful art is indeed a Christmas gift to treasure.'

Catherine Campbell, speaker and author of *Journey with Me*

'A Christmas feast of words and paintings to nourish your faith and warm your heart. Carve out some quiet, make a hot drink and take this book to your favourite reading chair – your experience of Advent will be all the richer for it. Amy's personal vignettes and profound spiritual insight, brought into vivid colour by her father's artwork, are a true gift for the season.'
Jo Swinney, author of *The Whole Christmas Story*

'There's something poignant in being reminded that Christmas is really about our everyday. Jesus' birth is a unique event, but the real miracle also comes in that God chose to inhabit our day-to-day reality, so God could experience what it is like for you to be you and me to be me, in all of our brokenness and vulnerability. Amy Boucher Pye's reflections are a glorious mixture of how the "perfect Christmas" is simply not achievable for us, but it is in the everyday stories where we see that we are blessed, loved and indeed hallowed by God. Amy's honesty about her own experiences and that of her family, including an impromptu mouse, brings the reality of Christmas to life, and this will resonate with so many of us.'
Rt Revd Rob Wickham, Bishop of Edmonton

Celebrating Christmas

Embracing joy through art and reflections

Reflections by
Amy Boucher Pye

Illustrations by
Leo Boucher

15 The Chambers, Vineyard
Abingdon OX14 3FE
brf.org.uk

Bible Reading Fellowship is a charity (233280)
and company limited by guarantee (301324),
registered in England and Wales

ISBN 978 1 80039 051 5
First published 2021
10 9 8 7 6 5 4 3 2 1 0
All rights reserved

Acknowledgements
Scripture quotations are taken from The Holy Bible, New International Version
(Anglicised edition) copyright © 1979, 1984, 2011 by Biblica. Used by permission of
Hodder & Stoughton Publishers, a Hachette UK company. All rights reserved. 'NIV' is
a registered trademark of Biblica. UK trademark number 1448790.

Every effort has been made to trace and contact copyright owners for material used
in this resource. We apologise for any inadvertent omissions or errors, and would ask
those concerned to contact us so that full acknowledgement can be made in the future.

A catalogue record for this book is available from the British Library

Printed by Gutenberg Press, Tarxien, Malta

To Mom:
keeper of Christmas,
creator of beauty,
woman of prayer
(Amy)

To Phyllis:
the key to each one
of my blessed memories
of Christmas
(Leo)

Contents

3 He is Jesus!

4 God becomes man

Introduction

The Christmas memories come flooding back… Enjoying the moments on my cousins' farm as we embark on a hayride in the snow-covered fields. Examining the gifts underneath the Christmas tree, checking the tags and wondering what could be in the ones bearing my name. Savouring the first bite of a seasonal treat. Experiencing the joy of singing Christmas carols together, the music moving us to praise God.

Christmas is a season to be celebrated, and my father and I hope that this book will accompany you, through words and images, as you ponder the wonder of God with us. Of Jesus being born as a baby, entering the world in humble and fragile circumstances, the miracle of God coming to earth. Our hope is that you'll be strengthened in your faith in the one who redeems, saves and makes all things new.

We've divided *Celebrating Christmas* into four sections, which you can dip into with a hot beverage while sitting by some sparkly lights during the twelve days of Christmas, or use during Advent as a Christmas-themed resource.

In part 1 we explore the cultural expressions of Christmas – the symbols that pop up all around us in December (or before). We can plumb many of these for rich spiritual meaning.

In part 2 we move to the joys and sorrows of Christmas. In our fallen world, we won't always experience the picture-book image of smiling faces gathered round a bounteous Christmas feast. We might feel the emptiness of someone missing or we might experience sadness over relational strife. Jesus was born precisely to give us hope in times like these.

Part 3 celebrates Jesus, as we select six of the biblical names for this baby born to be King. He truly is the 'reason for the season' and we delight to immerse ourselves in some of his attributes and character.

In part 4 we move to the nativity story itself, as told in the gospels of Luke and Matthew. As the story reaches its climax, we remember what the fuss is truly about – the miracle of new life, of God who becomes one of us. God revealed himself to us through his Son, Jesus, and he continues to show himself to us today through his indwelling in his followers and through the gift of his Holy Spirit. Entering into the story of the birth of Jesus again will bring us joy, faith, hope and love.

My dad and I would like to thank those at BRF: Karen Laister, for the initial idea for this book; Olivia Warburton, for how she's shepherded it through the publishing process with grace and panache; Daniele Och, for his editorial and production skills; Alison Beek, for her design talents; and Eley McAinsh, for spreading the word. We're also grateful for Tanya Marlow, Amy Scott Robinson, Penelope Swithinbank and Amy Young, for their insightful comments during the writing process, and for our family on both sides of the Atlantic, who have cheered us along each step of the way.

We pray that you'll be refreshed, inspired and encouraged as you enter these pages, which we hope will be a gift to you. May you experience peace and joy as you ponder the mystery of Jesus, God incarnate.

Amy Boucher Pye

Part 1
Symbols of Christmas

When we think of Christmas, images might pop into our minds of Christmas trees and decorations, carollers at the door, mulled wine and rich baked treats. So powerful are these evocative symbols of Christmas that sometimes they can overpower the true meaning of the holiday. Let's take a closer look.

1

The light in the darkness

Ahush descends as the lights are switched off. The congregation is bubbling with anticipation. A young child says, 'It's dark!' to muted laughter. We watch as the vicar lights the candle held by the person at the end of the row, and they light the candle next to them, and so on. Little glowing circles move down the rows until all the candles are lit and, faces aglow, we marvel at the beauty of light dispelling the darkness.

At the beginning of Advent, our church holds a service with Christingles, a symbol created with oranges and candles in 18th-century Germany to help children understand how Jesus is the light of the world. The flames dotted around the congregation speak of God's love dwelling in his children through his Spirit and Son, a mystery made possible because Jesus came to earth as a baby.

Light is warming, comforting and heralding, and God as the source of all light is a rich theme in the Bible. Indeed, light is the first thing that God creates in the Genesis account – even before the sun (Genesis 1:3–4). God then reveals himself as a light to his people, such as when he appeared to Moses 'in flames of fire from within a bush' (Exodus 3:2) or as a bright cloud or a pillar of fire (see Exodus 13:21–22).

In the New Testament, Matthew in his gospel says that Jesus fulfils Isaiah's prophecy that 'the people living in darkness have seen a great light; on those living in the land of the shadow of death a light has dawned' (Matthew 4:16). We might feel overcome by the darkness around us – the diseases, betrayals and injustices – but God shines his light on us through Jesus.

Similarly, John starts off his gospel with an affirmation of Jesus being the light of life: 'In him was life, and that life was the light of all mankind. The light shines in the darkness, and the darkness has not overcome it' (John 1:4–5). We live in a world permeated by darkness, but the black clouds and oppressive sense of nothingness will not win out against the light.

As you light your Advent candles, Christingles or other festive sparklers, ponder the glory and power of light – and of Jesus, the light who has come into the world.

Jesus, you bring light and life. As I yield to you, your presence within me burns away that which is not holy. Help me to welcome your clarifying light, that I might be free of any sin that clings. May your light within be a gentle and welcoming beacon, a signal in these dark times of a safe haven. Amen

2

The tree of life

I try to sleep, but my coughing keeps me up. Finally the exhaustion takes over and I fall asleep. In the morning I awaken to my mother's call, and when I walk into the living room I have a shock – the Christmas tree is gone.

When I was a child, each December I'd cough my way through the night. One evening my mother was out ten-pin bowling when a friend mentioned how they'd had to get rid of their Christmas tree because of their son's allergies. When my mother relayed the story to my dad, they realised the source of my cough. That very night, even though it was late, they removed the ornaments and lights, needles shedding as they threw the tree out into the snow. My cough disappeared and as a family we embraced the tradition of an artificial tree.

We may have missed the enticing smell of a newly cut tree, but we enjoyed the beauty and symbolism nonetheless. This tradition is broadly understood to go back to Martin Luther in 16th-century Germany, when one night the stars shining among some evergreen trees sparked wonder and praise within him. To recreate the scene for his family he cut down a tree and added lighted candles.[1]

Trees play an important role in the Bible, and in the Old Testament a tree-related prophecy alludes to the birth of Jesus: 'A shoot will come up from the stump of Jesse; from his roots a Branch will bear fruit' (Isaiah 11:1). Isaiah spoke these words to give hope to God's people when they faced enemies and exile. But another rich level of meaning is the Branch being the Messiah, Jesus Christ. The stump of Jesse may have appeared dead; after all, Jesse was the father of King David and this royal line all but vanished in significance. But this ancestry would eventually bring forth life through the God who became man. Jesus, son of David, would become the King of kings.

This Christmas, consider taking some time to read through Isaiah 11 while you gaze at a Christmas tree – artificial or not. Consider how a Christmas tree is cut off from its root and thus drops its needles throughout the season. Are there areas in your life where you feel cut off from God, your root? How might he set you into some rich soil to bring these areas back to life?

Creator God, thank you for filling the earth with trees, which give us shelter from the scorching sun and become a shield from the rain. Lord Jesus, thank you for being the branch to whom we are connected, the vine through which we receive sustenance and life. May your Spirit flow through us, bringing renewal and new life, as we celebrate your birth. Amen

3

Stockings of delight

We're bursting to share our news. Wondering if my husband being on the phone call with me and my parents will be a tip-off, I barrel ahead: 'So we have a question to ask you. Mom, will you be willing to make another Christmas stocking for us?'

We listen to the pregnant pause and then hear the joy in their voices: 'You're expecting!'

We are indeed, and enjoy sharing this exciting news through asking my mother to make one of her intricately embroidered Christmas stockings to add to the two that we hang over the fireplace each year. The gift of new life is so meaningful to anticipate at Christmas.

The tradition of Christmas stockings is said to hail back to St Nicholas, who was born in AD280 in what is modern-day Turkey. A wealthy man who dedicated his life to serving God and others, he loved to give gifts but wanted to remain anonymous while doing so. When he heard that three young women were made destitute after their mother died and their father through his grief squandered their money, Nicholas decided to help to rebuild their dowries. Over the course of three nights he threw a bag of gold down the chimney, which landed in the socks hanging to dry on the mantel. The women were touched and cheered by this amazing gift of generosity, meaning they'd now have the means to marry and start their own families.

This story of St Nicholas eventually turned into the cultural phenomenon of Santa Claus, with 'santa' the Spanish word for saint and 'Claus' a variation of Nicholas. The red suit and twinkle in his eye came later, but Santa started off as a benevolent man who gives gifts in the middle of the night.

Some families infuse the cultural stories around Christmas with a distinctly Christian theme, such as those who hang a stocking for Jesus along with the other stockings for family members. During Advent, each person gives spiritual gifts to Jesus, noting them on slips of paper. They could be an act of kindness, such as a brother looking out for his sister at school or a parent saving some money to give some non-perishables to the local food bank. On Christmas, when the family opens their stockings, they first read out together the gifts that they've given Jesus, rejoicing in the way they've shared his love.

Imagine you're following the stocking-for-Jesus practice this year. What act of kindness could you do today? How could you clothe yourself with 'compassion, kindness, humility, gentleness and patience' (Colossians 3:12)?

Lord Jesus Christ, you gave of yourself that I might have life, and life eternal. Spark in my heart a deep sense of gratitude for the many gifts I enjoy. Help me to give of myself and my bounty, that others would know your love through me. Amen

4

Giving and receiving

The snowflakes melt on my cheeks in the short walk from our front door to the car, which Dad warms up for us. The sky is dark. I take care not to slip on the icy path. We kids and Dad wait for Mom, the one in our family who is usually ready first. What's she doing? We guess she's playing Santa, but we're not completely sure, secretly hoping that the fairy tale is true.

We wait, stomachs churning. There she is – now we can go to church. We join in the prayers and sing the carols, but all the time we wait, wondering what presents we'll find under the tree. We shuffle in our seats, waiting. We follow the familiar rise and fall of the prayers, waiting.

And then church is over and homeward we go, the moment nearly here. The weeks of asking for the longed-for presents – will our hopes come true? Will I receive the Barbie camper van I've been pining for? When it's my turn to open a present, I grab the biggest one, which is just the right size. Heart pounding, I rip the paper and exclaim, 'You got it for me!', holding up the pink van for my family to see.

Today those memories cheer me, for my parents lavished us with love and some pretty wonderful gifts. I'm aware, however, that not everyone holds memories of such an outpouring. If that's the case, we can ask God to resymbolise presents for us, whether through the giving or the receiving of them. We can funnel our creativity into finding just the right gift for someone, which of course might be something that we don't spend a lot of money on – a meal we make, a poem we write, a woodcarving we create. Jesus, the greatest gift of all, can change the way we view presents.

We give because he first gave to us: 'Every good and perfect gift is from above, coming down from the Father of the heavenly lights, who does not change like shifting shadows' (James 1:17). This Advent and Christmas season, could you share with someone else, such as through a financial contribution or a secret gift?

Christ Jesus, thank you for humbling yourself and coming to live as one of us. We celebrate your birth and your life, for you bring us freedom and hope. Increase our ability to receive from you and from others – open our hearts and our hands to your bounty. And help us to give to you and to others, sharing from the wonders of your love and your life. Amen

5

Music, the language of praise

I note that we'll be singing 'Away in a manger', and my heart swells as I think back to joining in with this carol as a child in snowy Minnesota. Now I'm spending my first Christmas in England as my new husband and I seek to create traditions for our life together. I don't reckon on choking back the tears because of a simple Christmas carol at the all-age service. But as the organ rings out, I think, 'That's not the right tune!' The realisation hits me in the gut that life really is different now – even the Christmas carols aren't the same.

Music can touch us deeply because it can whizz past our rational minds to sink into our hearts and imaginations. The refrain from a carol or a song can instantly transport us to another place and time as we remember a favourite person who loved it or special times singing round the piano. More than just lifting our spirits, music can help us lose ourselves in adoration of our God – the God-in-three-persons, one of whom came to earth as a baby.

Praising God through song appears in various places in the Bible, especially in the Psalms. We might think that the angels sang in praise when they announced the birth of Jesus to the shepherds. Luke's gospel, however, doesn't specify that: 'Suddenly a great company of the heavenly host appeared with the angel, praising God and *saying*, "Glory to God in the highest heaven, and on earth peace to those on whom his favour rests"' (Luke 2:13–14, emphasis mine). We probably have in mind Charles Wesley's hymn 'Hark the herald angels sing', which he actually wrote as 'Hark! How all the welkin rings, glory to the King of Kings', with 'welkin' meaning the heavens. But to Wesley's dismay, his friend George Whitefield reworked the song, and the newer rendition became popular.[2] Perhaps, however, the best version has endured, for angels sing elsewhere in the Bible.

When we worship through song, we can unite our emotions and thoughts in praise and adoration. New tunes can become familiar and bring to mind different memories – such as my reaction now when I hear 'Away in a manger', having lived in Britain for over two decades. I smile to remember my daughter decked out in a Santa hat, singing the song with verve while carolling in the community.

Why not choose one particular Christmas carol to focus on this year as you celebrate our Saviour's birth?

'Be near me, Lord Jesus, I ask you to stay
close by me forever, and love me, I pray.
Bless all the dear children in your tender care,
and fit us for heaven to live with you there.'

6

Depictions of the real

We can credit Francis of Assisi, known for loving nature and animals, for creating the first nativity scene in 1223. Longing that those in the Italian village of Greccio would experience the wonder of the story of Jesus' birth, he created a cave scene with hay, an ox and a donkey. Welcoming the villagers to gaze on the scene, he told the story of Mary and Joseph arriving in Bethlehem without anywhere to stay.

Nativity sets have become a special part of the season, with many people adding the straw and the various figures, one by one, during Advent. The nativity sets aren't always the most accurate, though; for example, the magi visited Jesus when he was a toddler, not just after the shepherds heard the good news. And the family probably wouldn't have been staying in a barn-like structure but would have sheltered in the lower half of a home, where the animals were housed at night.

But the imperfect things we create, such as nativity sets, can give us insights into the real. That is, as we gaze on them, perhaps in an attitude of praying to God, we can understand more deeply the mystery of the God who came to earth as a baby. We might, like the Italian villagers, imagine ourselves as Mary or Joseph in a chilly dwelling, animals around us, as we ponder the love of these new parents for a fragile, helpless baby.

My favourite nativity set is one that my dad created out of wood many years ago, which he's depicted in this painting. I love its simplicity – it's merely a block of wood with the three figures cut out of thin pieces of wood stained in a dark colour. Sometimes when we strip things down to the essentials, we realise anew what is important.

This year as you move from Advent to Christmas, try to keep focused on the main thing – the birth of the Son of God. Perhaps as you add the figures to a nativity set, with the joy of placing Jesus in the manger on Christmas Eve, your sense of wonder and gratitude will grow all the more too.

Lord Jesus Christ, you are the centre of our celebrations at Christmas. We can easily get sidetracked with all of the trappings of the holiday – the shopping and planning, parties and festivities, baking and cooking. Help us to focus on you, that we might never lose our sense of wonder, awe and gratitude. Amen

Part 2

The joys and sorrows of Christmas

We all long to enjoy a special Christmas, shared with loved ones, worshipping the babe born to be King. We may, however, find ourselves alone, in conflict with others or with the holiday just not as we imagined. Here we explore the joys and sorrows of Christmas in a broken world – exactly why Jesus came to earth!

7

Gathering to worship at Christmas

The church darkened, the candlelight flickers from the eaves and candelabras. The crib scene is illuminated; the Christmas tree sparkles at the back. I inhale deeply, gratitude spreading throughout as I anticipate my favourite church service of the year – the one at 11.00 pm on Christmas Eve. Our celebratory Christmas Eve feast, shared with others from our church and the community, has just finished, and I'm glowing with the warmth of having welcomed others to experience the traditions I grew up with in America. As I listen to the evocative flute solo, I release my mind from my to-do lists and give myself to the worship of Jesus, the God who became a baby.

I look around our community in north London, gathered in the soft light, seeing faces of those who've travelled with us for many years and those just joining. I give thanks for the woman who faithfully nursed her mother through dementia, serving her while grieving for all that she was losing, day by day. I notice the adult children who are with us as they visit their parents, returning home as they make their new home in the world. I ask God to help me love one whom I find difficult when she shares her opinions over my husband's leadership of the church. And I see those whom I know have come early to set up and who are still monitoring the candles overhead to make sure we don't have any mishaps.

This is church – the beautiful, broken, loving, hurting, rejoicing group of people, all made in God's image and beloved by him. This gift of church is something we enjoy only because Jesus came to earth as a baby, living and dying as one of us and then being resurrected by his Father. He's now the head of the church, and we are his body, as the apostle Paul wrote to the church (that is, the people) at Ephesus: 'And God placed all things under his feet and appointed him to be head over everything for the church, which is his body, the fullness of him who fills everything in every way' (Ephesians 1:22–23).

Why not take some moments to ponder the gift of church as you pray for your church – those you love seeing regularly and those who send you to your knees in prayer. May we accept this rich but sometimes messy gift with grace, gratitude and joy.

*Christ Jesus, you are the head of the church and we are your body.
Father God, you deign to use us as your feet and your fingers!
Strengthening Spirit, you help us to love those whom we enjoy
and those we find irritating as you equip us to share your good
news of great joy. May we experience your love more fully this
Christmas so that we can extend it even more generously to those
in the church – and those we hope will join us. Amen*

8

The body of Christ

I gasp when I hear that my prayer partner has spoken out against our vicar – my husband. When I learn that she's one of a group expressing their views of discontent, I feel like I've been punched in the stomach. Although I haven't known her long, I've shared with her deep and intimate things. On this day of piercing news, I don't realise that for a long time afterwards I will feel betrayed, hurt and wounded.

Perhaps you've experienced something similar when someone let you down. If you're human and have attended church for a length of time, I'm guessing you too will have felt disappointment, weariness, anger and pain because of something that's happened at God's house.

Church communities don't always match the idyllic image we hold, such as the one depicted in this evocative painting. This little church, enveloped by the branches and cushioned by snow, reflects the safety and cosiness we long for.

Although church can be a place of pain, it can also be a haven for joy and communion, for peace and fellowship, for wonder and relating. After all, we as the church embody the presence of Christ. How is that so? Because Jesus came to earth as a baby to usher in a new kingdom through his death and resurrection, he now fills us with his presence and thus we find union not only with him but also with others.

Jesus asked his Father for this union for us when he prayed for his disciples before he died: 'I pray also… that all of them may be one, Father, just as you are in me and I am in you' (John 17:20–21). When Jesus dwells in us, living within us, he gives us the power to love those in our churches, warts and all. Even as they too can love us with all of our imperfections and failings.

May this Christmas season be a rich time of unity with your fellow believers, when the shared joy over the birth of our Saviour brings hope, reconciliation and peace.

Father God, you sent your Son to earth as a baby, that he might live as one of us. How you must ache for the way your children are bound up by pain and recrimination. Thank you that you want to relieve us of this heartache. As we turn to you for comfort and help, foster unity and peace in our places of worship, bringing healing and release where there has been hurt and betrayal. May we sense your calming presence in our lives this day. Amen

9

Blue Christmas

I look across the table at my new husband as he valiantly tries to eat my first attempt at homemade chicken noodle soup. It's Christmas Eve, and I've utterly failed to make the (to me) traditional feast – the gloopy noodles with watery stock are nearly inedible. Looking for some comfort, I call my family across the Atlantic in Minnesota, but hearing their loving voices touches off even more sadness within me. As I express my regret of not being with them at Christmas, my dad says, 'Amy, you longed to marry and now you have. It's right that you're there with Nicholas.' He's wise and gentle, even if at that moment I struggle to listen.

That first Christmas in England is the closest that I've experienced to having a 'blue Christmas'. I'm aware, however, that the pain and heartache of others may be far more intense. For instance, your table might never again include that special someone sitting at it. Living in a world marred by sin, disease and death, we'll all have some kind of reckoning with a blue Christmas at some point.

Some churches host a 'longest night' service (calling it that instead of 'blue Christmas' to get away from the associations with the Elvis Presley song), where people can celebrate Christmas without any forced jollity. Instead of having to bury their feelings of pain and anguish, they can express them to God through the reflective singing and prayers. Attending such a service doesn't require a tragedy either; it can be an oasis of calm amid a too-busy time of parties, baking and gift exchanges.

God welcomes the cries of lament from his people; indeed, Jesus wept angry tears at the tomb of Lazarus. The season of Advent can actually help us to lament, because it reminds us to wait for the second coming of Christ, when God will come and relieve us of our pain: '"He will wipe every tear from their eyes. There will be no more death" or mourning or crying or pain, for the old order of things has passed away' (Revelation 21:4). Celebrating Christmas through tears – 'happy Christmas anyway' – can mean acknowledging that we hold the answer to our lament through the gift of Christ. Even as we wait for his coming again.

If you're feeling low and broken this year, I pray you'll find comfort and hope in the God who comes to brush away the tears from your eyes. As you release your pain to him, may you experience a deep sense of love, peace and even joy.

Loving Lord, how you must grieve at the horrors that we encounter, whether through natural disaster, human-made conflict or our own errant behaviour. Deal with us ever so mercifully. Bind up our wounds and give us the strength to worship as you renew our stores of hope. Amen

10

Joy in the wilderness

On this Christmas morning, I look round the front room of a friend of a friend, wishing we were back in north London. Although our vicarage there is decorated to the hilt, we are on England's south coast because my husband has been signed off from his church work. His mother's death a couple of months before set off some family issues and has brought about a stint of depression, meaning no shared Christmas with our church family. I feel the need to be strong for our kids, ensuring their Christmas isn't tinged with sadness, but the lack of decorations as a backdrop to our opening of the Christmas presents adds another layer of weariness and grief. I feel like we're wandering in the wilderness, not knowing how long the mental-health issues will last or how the family stuff will work out. I breathe a prayer asking God to give us joy and to lead us out of these hard and rocky times.

The Israelites faced 40 years of wandering in the wilderness. While there, God through Moses gave his people a set of feasts and festivals they were to observe at certain points of the year to remember his goodness to them. Interestingly, he outlined one festival that they would observe only *after* they'd entered the promised land, the feast of the firstfruits: 'When you enter the land I am going to give you and you reap its harvest, bring to the priest a sheaf of the first grain you harvest' (Leviticus 23:10). God's issuing of this feast meant that they would grow food that Pharaoh couldn't claim. He was promising that they'd indeed make it to the promised land.[3]

For me on that Christmas Day, finding joy in the wilderness meant hoping for the future without knowing how we'd travel there. And on a smaller level, it meant relinquishing the need for a beautiful setting as the backdrop of our celebrations. As I leaned into God's love, I received the joy of joining dear friends who welcomed us to their family Christmas lunch, complete with a massive turkey with all of the trimmings and riotous games of charades.

Whatever your circumstances, whether you feel you're living in the wilderness or you've reached the promised land – or somewhere in between – may you know God's provision and care in the today as you hope for tomorrow.

Creator God, how you must have longed that your children could have avoided the 40 years in the wilderness. But you never left them on their own. When I'm feeling lost and wandering, reveal your presence so that I don't lose hope. Guide me to the land of feasting, that I might enjoy your good gifts and live with you forever. Amen

11

Giving from what we've received

She stands outside our vicarage door, arms laden with bags. 'Hello, lovely Amy!' she says with her Italian lilt. Every Christmas she comes bearing gifts for people in the parish, including tasty boxes of panettone bread and a bottle of wine for the vicar. We chat, with her sharing about her son and grandchildren, and I thank her for her kindness while inviting her to our carol service. After closing the door, I call out to my kids, 'It was Carlotta! Come and see what she brought.' They bound downstairs, wondering what sort of mix it will be this time.

Carlotta loves to give, and we love to receive and pass along her gifts. But I have learnt to vet the offerings. As the kids and I sort through the bags, we notice some scribbled-out sell-by dates on box after box of mince pies. I remark that it's good I don't like mince pies or I'd be tempted to taste and see just how out of date they are. Part of the adventure of receiving these offerings-to-the-vicarage is wondering what Carlotta will come up with next.

Christmas is a wonderful time to serve others and share from our bounty – perhaps without passing along past-it items! We, like Carlotta, might love giving or we might enjoy serving in other ways, as depicted in this painting. Or we might simply know that God wants us to be generous, however imperfectly we do so.

Early on in God's journey with his people, God commanded them through Moses to look outside of their own needs and to share with others. God instituted part of his law, which he designed for them to flourish, to include looking out for others: 'There will always be poor people in the land. Therefore, I command you to be open-handed towards your fellow Israelites who are poor and needy in your land' (Deuteronomy 15:11).

How could you follow God's instructions this Christmas? Here are a few ideas to spread the love of Christ as we celebrate his birthday:

1 Volunteer at a local food bank or homeless shelter.

2 Instead of selling an item you no longer need, make it available for free.

3 Spend an evening scrolling through your social media account, but do so while praying for the people and needs you discern.

4 Text someone and arrange a time to chat on the phone (or take a risk and call them, unannounced, like we used to do before mobile phones).

Lord Jesus Christ, as a baby you were a refugee in Egypt and your family depended on the kindness of strangers. Spark love and generosity in my heart, that I might give to others what you have so freely already shared with me. Amen

12

Christmas in the city

With the late-afternoon darkness settling in, I emerge from the Tube station to a sensory overload. People bustle about, loaded down by their purchases; the smells of roasted nuts waft around me; I hear the rumble of a bus rushing past. I walk along, moving away from the hyperactivity of Oxford Street as I follow the Christmas lights overhead. Momentarily forgetting I'm surrounded by pedestrians, I gaze at the sparkling creations of light. As I take in the sight of angels with their powerful wings flying over me, I have a flash of insight – real angels, however they actually appear, are in the heavenlies even now. I'm surrounded not only by these amazing beings that God created but by the cloud of witnesses described in Hebrews 12:1. The commotion continues around me, but in that moment I receive a gift of wonder and awe.

Revelling in God's creation in the midst of the city might seem strange, as many people view urban centres as dirty, violent places from which they wish to escape.

God, however, loves them. As he revealed to the beloved apostle John, his heavenly city will descend to the new earth where he will live with his people:

> Then I saw 'a new heaven and a new earth,' for the first heaven and the first earth had passed away, and there was no longer any sea. I saw the Holy City, the new Jerusalem, coming down out of heaven from God, prepared as a bride beautifully dressed for her husband. And I heard a loud voice from the throne saying, 'Look! God's dwelling-place is now among the people, and he will dwell with them. They will be his people, and God himself will be with them and be their God. "He will wipe every tear from their eyes. There will be no more death" or mourning or crying or pain, for the old order of things has passed away.'
>
> REVELATION 21:1–4

God dwelling with his people – this is the reality of the heavens and earth to come and is the amazing truth we celebrate at Christmas. Jesus was born a baby and became a man who lived with us, died for our sins and welcomes us into God's holy city. He's with us now in our brokenness and our beauty, and he'll be with us forevermore.

God of all mercy and grace, open our minds and our hearts to receive a glimpse of you and of your kingdom of grace. Help us to know that what is unseen is yet real – to hold on to hope and faith that what you promise will come true. Increase our longing for the day of the new heavens and the new earth, when you wipe away all of our tears and the old order of things vanishes forever. Amen

Part 3

He is Jesus!

The God who became man, born of Mary in the manger, is Jesus. His attributes are many, giving us a rich feast to enjoy as we consider his various names at Christmas. Here we explore Jesus as creator, God with us, light of the world, lamb of God, King of kings and the bright morning star. Enjoy!

13

Creator God

North London is a hive of activity this December, but I've planned my walk to the nearby brook so that I can go without seeing anyone for a few minutes. I take in the beauty around me – the water gurgles; the bare trees form a spindly canopy over me; the scampering squirrels make me smile. As I marvel at this pocket of beauty so near the metropolis, I think about God as creator and the Genesis account. And I ponder *Jesus* as creator.[4]

It may feel jarring to us, but Jesus plays a role in creation, because God is three persons in one – the Father, Son and Holy Spirit. John opens his gospel with this truth, echoing the words in Genesis: 'In the beginning was the Word, and the Word was with God, and the Word was God' (John 1:1). Jesus is the Word, the *logos* in Greek. 'He was with God in the beginning' (v. 2). He was there; he and the Spirit together with God (with the Spirit mentioned in Genesis 1:2: 'and the Spirit of God was hovering over the waters').

As John continues, note the role of Jesus as creator: 'Through him all things were made; without him nothing was made that has been made. In him was life, and that life was the light of all mankind' (vv. 3–4). John affirms that all things were made through Christ! He's there giving his life as the light of all people.

Other passages in the New Testament also point to Jesus as creator. Why does this matter? One reason is that it helps us pause and give thanks that he who was above creation and part of the act of creating yet humbled himself to become a created being – and even a baby born in very ordinary circumstances – so that he could relate to us, bring us salvation and dwell within us. Another reason is that Jesus is all about redemption. His miracles and healings put things back the way they were before sin entered the world. Through his presence today he continues to bring joy, healing, peace and restoration.[5]

All creation praises God the creator – the Father who initiated the act of creation, the Son by whom all things were created and the Spirit who hovered over the waters before the world came into being. All glory and praise to God!

*Lord Jesus, expand my mind and my heart to understand
even more what it means that in you all things hold together.
You hold together not only the tiny atoms, but the whole universe.
And you love me deeply and gently. Help me to praise and worship
you more and more. Amen*

✳ 14 ✳

God with us

I know the script, having seen many nativity plays. I can picture a cute little girl as Mary who holds a doll while standing next to a shell-shocked Joseph. But I'm not prepared for the rush of emotions as I'm decked out as an adult Mary with Nicholas next to me as Joseph. I gaze at our infant son who has been cast in the role of Jesus and feel a powerful surge of love for our Lord along with a new appreciation for his earthly parents. Just as our son could disrupt this performance with his cries of hunger or tiredness, so too, I consider, could Jesus have been unpredictable for Mary and Joseph. He was a wriggly baby, full of needs and potential, but he was also God. My sleep-addled brain tries to understand this mystery of God in human form – God with us.

Jesus being born was prophesied through Isaiah, whom Matthew quotes in his gospel: 'All this took place to fulfil what the Lord had said through the prophet: "The virgin will conceive and give birth to a son, and they will call him Immanuel" (which means "God with us")' (Matthew 1:22–23). This term 'Immanuel' appears in the New Testament only here; translated literally it means 'with us is God'.

Immanuel is God in the form of a baby – an actual child who hungered and slept and probably disrupted many a night for Joseph and Mary. God as Jesus experienced what we encounter, such as feeling dirt in his toes, enjoying the companionship of friends or knowing the satisfaction of a good meal. Jesus came to give his life as a sacrifice that we might enjoy our life with God. Because he was born as a baby, specifically in Bethlehem as we see in this imaginative painting, we can be assured that he will never leave us.

One way to sift through the layers of meaning of Jesus as Immanuel is to picture yourself holding Jesus in your arms. We know that Jesus was a baby – a helpless, crying baby – but have we so ingested the image of the man-child Jesus with a halo, staring at us beatifically, that we find it hard to visualise him as a real, live baby? Take a few moments to imagine Jesus in this way. What does he look like? What's he doing? How do you feel? Perhaps as you pray, like Mary you can ponder all these things in your heart.

Lord Jesus, we welcome you! You are the God who lives with us, the one who will never leave us. Help us to know afresh what that means. As we consider the miracle of your birth, fill us with your presence and your love. And help us to reach out to a world aching to hear your message of good news. Amen

15

Light of the world

Before going to bed, I tramp down the stairs to get a glass of water. Deciding I'd better make sure the garden door is locked, I turn on the light in the living room and to my surprise and dismay glimpse a mouse scurrying across the room. The sudden light sends this unwanted creature into the bowels of the Victorian vicarage.

As we noted in our first reading, Jesus is the light who dispels the darkness; his light brings heat, life and comfort. Jesus called himself the light of the world during one of the important Jewish feasts, the Feast of Tabernacles.

At the end of the first day of the feast, lamps are lit in the temple, which burn throughout this seven-day celebration of God leading his people out of the wilderness. Then at the end of the festival, as the lamps are extinguished, Jesus announces: 'I am the light of the world. Whoever follows me will never walk in darkness, but will have the light of life' (John 8:12). Here he's signalling that God's presence – that which appeared in the clouds and the fire to Moses and God's people – now dwells in him. The lamp in the temple may have been extinguished, but he as God's light shines forth. Jesus in his message declares that he's the Messiah who has come to save the hurting and the lost. Some are intrigued by Jesus, but the religious leaders become incensed. Jesus the light can also divide.[6]

Take a few moments to ponder Jesus as the light of the world, making the darkness flee. You might want to take some time considering this vivid painting, where we glimpse the light of Jesus warming and brightening the horizon as the sun rises. Perhaps you could pray for someone who hasn't encountered the light of Christ. Or maybe you'd like to ask Christ to show you any places of darkness you might be tempted to move towards when you're feeling fearful or hurt. Ask God through his Spirit to shine his light on you and those you love, that you all would stay faithful during the periods of the night before you move into the warmth of the morning sunshine.

Jesus, light of the world, you send the darkness scurrying away. Shine your light into my heart and mind, that I might follow you with love, consistency, passion and joy. Help me to cling to the light when I'm tempted to dip my toes into any of the darkness that I find enticing. I want to stay close to you, Lord, that I too might share your compelling, warming light with others. Amen

16

Lamb of God

Our weekend at a retreat centre in Devon surprises us, not only for the snow-storm that cocoons us together for an extra day but also for the opportunity to witness some lambs being born. We gather in the barn, our breath turning into misty clouds as we watch the miracle of new life in all its messy glory. To our amazement, minutes after the mother cleans up her baby, the newborn lamb totters around on its wobbly legs.

Lambs are special in the Bible; they are seen as a symbol of innocence and gentle-ness. And Jesus as the lamb of God is rooted in an Old Testament practice. Twice daily in worship the Israelites would sacrifice a lamb as an offering to ask God to forgive their sins (see Exodus 29:38–42). Later in the Old Testament, Isaiah's prophecy hints that the Messiah will be the ultimate lamb offered as a sacrifice to bear our sins: 'He was led like a lamb to the slaughter, and as a sheep before its shearers is silent, so he did not open his mouth… he will bear their iniquities' (Isaiah 53:7, 11).

In the days after Jesus' resurrection, that very passage of scripture was what the Ethiopian eunuch was studying when Philip met him on the road. By explaining how Jesus fulfilled Isaiah's prophecy, Philip shared with him the good news of how Jesus saves people from their sins. The man was so taken by Philip's testimony that when he saw some water by the side of the road, he asked to be baptised. Philip did so, and they rejoiced (see Acts 8:32–39).

Considering Jesus as the lamb of God might be something we do more naturally at Easter than at Christmas, but our nativity sets can be helpful in focusing our minds and hearts. Of course, these groupings of figurines might not get everything right in terms of Jesus' birth. After all, the gospel stories don't specifically mention if any animals were present, just that he was lying in a manger (see Luke 2). All the same, if you have a nativity set, why not hold one of its little lambs as you ponder before God how Jesus offers us the gift of salvation and how his sacrifice wipes our record of wrongdoing clean? That's the best present we'll ever receive.

Lord Jesus Christ, thank you for taking on the sin of the world. Indeed, thank you for washing me clean of my wrongdoing. As we celebrate your birth, help me to consider the cost of the gift that you have given me as you increase my gratitude and devotion to you. May I serve you with joy and share with others your message of peace and love. Amen

17

King of kings

I take in my surroundings, noticing the peeling paint in the town hall, its grandeur wearing with the years. I'm seated with a group of diverse people, most of whom speak different languages. As we follow the lead of the government official, we hold the text in front of us as we pledge allegiance to the Queen. I don't feel any great rush of emotions as I become her subject, perhaps because I'm directing a lot of energy towards trying to sit comfortably on the hard bench while I'm eight months pregnant with our second child.

I'm aware, however, of my lingering ambivalence about authority. Although I respect and admire Queen Elizabeth, I find bowing to those born into a position of influence challenging. After all, history shows us so many examples of power being wielded to fuel egos while ignoring the needs of the poor and downtrodden.

After Mary travelled uncomfortably in response to the edict of Caesar Augustus, Jesus was born into a royal position that far surpassed that of the Roman emperor. For

Jesus has the highest title ever to be conferred: King of kings. But he's an altogether different kind of king than hapless or evil rulers on earth. Instead, he embodies the qualities of the king noted in Psalm 72: he's endowed with justice, judges the people in righteousness, defends the afflicted, saves the children of the needy, crushes the oppressor, endures as long as the sun, rules from sea to sea, delivers the needy who cry out, takes pity on the weak and rescues them from oppression and violence (Psalm 72:1–2, 4–5, 8, 12–14).

Wise men recognised his royal nature, as reflected in this painting. As they read the stars they understood that a king had been born. Risking the wrath of King Herod, a veritable killing machine, they asked where they could find Jesus so that they could worship him (see Matthew 2). Later Jesus as king rode a humble donkey for his triumphal entrance into Jerusalem, signalling that he was royalty with a difference (see Matthew 21). And in the times to come, as King of kings he'll ride in triumphantly on a white horse while wearing many crowns (see Revelation 19).

We who have the benefit of scripture and years of church history don't need a star in the east to understand that Jesus is King. We even have the Holy Spirit to help us to bow before him as we honour and praise this baby born to be King. I hope that I – and you – have no ambivalence about that.

Jesus, King of kings and Lord of lords. You are mighty and powerful; you are loving and humble. Help me to worship and serve you with gladness and a singleness of heart. Renew in me a sense of awe and wonder about how great you are. Amen

18

Morning star

'Whose idea was it to do this at night?' I mutter to myself. I'm weighed down by heavy packs while trudging along an eight-and-a-half-mile trail leading to Lake Superior in northern Minnesota. This is the final challenge of a canoe trip with friends, and I'm weary and bruised from stumbling over the vines embedded in the path. Because we've spread out over the trail, I'm alone and near tears. But when I reach a point where the woods open up to the night sky, I stop and look up, realising that the horizon has lightened. As I take in the shining moon and a particularly bright star nestled among others, I find myself enveloped in peace. I may have a couple more miles to complete, but the lights in the sky remind me that I'm not alone. Jesus is with me.

As we've seen, the Bible is rich in its imagery about Jesus, including Jesus being a bright morning star. In the Old Testament, God uses a sorcerer to give his message to a pagan king, saying, 'I see him, but not now; I behold him, but not near. A star will come out of Jacob; a sceptre will rise out of Israel' (Numbers 24:17). The prophecy in the original context probably points to King David, but it also alludes to Jesus the Messiah. We see its fulfilment in the last book of the Bible, when Jesus refers to himself as not only the heir of David but also the bright morning star: 'I, Jesus, have sent my angel to give you this testimony for the churches. I am the Root and the Offspring of David, and the bright Morning Star' (Revelation 22:16).

What the Bible calls the morning star is actually Venus, the second planet from the sun and our closest neighbour. As it can be glimpsed in the eastern sky before dawn, in Bible times people understood it as signalling that the sun would soon rise. Jesus appearing in the world indicates the breaking of a new dawn – an era of new life, freedom and fruitfulness. No longer will darkness infiltrate the earth, for God's light shines through his Son, Jesus.[7]

If you're in the northern hemisphere, it's easier to wake for the sunrise during Advent as it appears later than in the summer. Why not set aside some time to gaze at the morning skies, praising Jesus as our bright morning star?

Jesus, you are the bright morning star and you signal the hope of a new world. When I feel overwhelmed by the darkness that I experience and witness, give me the hope and assurance that you've not abandoned me or your world. Usher in your kingdom of goodness and light. Amen

Part 4

God becomes man

Our last seven reflections and paintings immerse us in the story of Jesus being born to Mary and Joseph. The gospel stories in Matthew and Luke may feel so familiar that we wonder if we can glean anything new. Just as God revealed himself to each of the people in this wonderful narrative, so does he make himself known to us. I invite you to turn the page with a sense of expectancy and awe.

19

On the journey

I pack our bags, eager to introduce my husband to a Christmas with my family in Minnesota. I feel the pressure of my long to-do list before we make our way to Heathrow and then to the middle of America. As I stress, I fret about delays, hoping that the impending snowstorm won't derail enjoyment of the traditions I grew up with, which I want to share with Nicholas. He in turn is bringing a Christmas cake and pudding to introduce some of the English customs dear to him. I ask God to quell my nerves as I pack the carefully wrapped presents in my suitcase.

The particular travel challenges we face differ from those of Mary and Joseph, who journeyed from Nazareth to Bethlehem, a trip of about 90 miles. They had to go because 'in those days Caesar Augustus issued a decree that a census should be taken of the entire Roman world' (Luke 2:1). Thus with the nine-month-pregnant Mary probably perched uncomfortably on a donkey, they made their way south along the flatlands by the Jordan River and then west up and down the hills surrounding Jerusalem before reaching Bethlehem. Travelling in the Judean desert during the winter, they would have experienced a drenching rain that would have soaked their woollen clothes and chilled them to the bone. When they reached the city of Joseph's ancestors, they couldn't even find a place to stay.[8]

At Christmas we celebrate the culmination of these gruelling travels – not only their physical journey but the amazing one of God becoming a man. What a wonderful mystery that God the Father would delight to send his beloved Son to live as one of us. To enter the messiness and beauty of our world. To heal and preach and teach, drawing many to himself and to the Father. And, of course, to die on a cross and rise to life that we too might live forever.

As you celebrate the birth of Jesus, ponder the physical journeys you've been on recently (or those you want to take) and consider what you experienced when you left the comfort of your home. How did the act of leaving change you? Think too of your spiritual movements, looking back over the past year. How are you moving towards – or away from – God?

Lord Jesus, thank you for humbling yourself to be born in that stable. Your name is above every name, but you didn't claim your rights. Instead you lowered yourself to the level of a servant. Help me to grasp this truth as I celebrate your birth. Journey with me and make me more open to the work of your Spirit, that I might be willing to travel where you gently lead me. Amen

20

O little town of Bethlehem

We load up the car with bedding, a cooler filled with food, and lots of presents. We're returning to the land of my mother – Iowa, the state below Minnesota – and along with my siblings I'm bursting with excitement. I love going to my cousins' farm for our yearly Christmas celebration. We'll hang out in the hayloft, enjoy our festive feast, help with the dishes and participate in what we kids see as the main event – the Christmas-present exchange. As I grab my pillow, I wonder how many cats live in the barn and hope I won't have nightmares about the bull in the last pen.

Although some people joke about Iowa because it has so much farmland, I always loved visiting because of the people there. I'd look forward to our gatherings of the maternal family, not only my mother's siblings and parents but her aunts and uncles and cousins too. While these Swiss-German descendants didn't favour showy emotional displays, I always knew they loved me.

Joseph and Mary needed to go back to the land of his ancestors, not for the happy reason of a family celebration but to be counted in the census. The Roman authorities wanted to know how many men they could conscript into their service (from which Jewish people were exempt) and also how many people they could tax.

And so Mary and Joseph returned to David's city, which fulfilled God's purposes of Jesus being born there, as foretold by the prophet Micah: 'But you, Bethlehem Ephrathah, though you are small among the clans of Judah, out of you will come for me one who will be ruler over Israel, whose origins are from of old, from ancient times' (Micah 5:2). Note how Matthew's gospel modifies the prophecy to reflect how the Messiah's birth brings greatness to this city: 'But you, Bethlehem, in the land of Judah, are by no means least among the rulers of Judah; for out of you will come a ruler who will shepherd my people Israel' (Matthew 2:6).

Take some time to consider your special places, whether from your childhood or later in life. How have those geographical locations – and the people therein – shaped and formed who you are today? You might also want to dream about where you'd like to visit next.

Jesus, son of David, your birth in Bethlehem fulfilled God's promises. Thank you for the places that are dear to me, whether I live there still or only travel there in my memories. Help me to bless these spaces and the people who live there as I share your love and light this Christmas season. Amen

21

Jesus is born!

I awake on Christmas morning, eager to share the day with my husband, three-year-old and the people at our church. I'm excited, but I'm also awash with a mixture of emotions. Although I'm pregnant, I mourn the baby who would have been born a week before, whom we lost to miscarriage. *How can I be so happy and grateful one moment*, I wonder, *and sad the next? Will our baby inside me be born a healthy child?*

When Mary gave birth to Jesus, she must have experienced a range of emotions too: 'While they were there [in Bethlehem], the time came for the baby to be born, and she gave birth to her firstborn, a son. She wrapped him in cloths and placed him in a manger, because there was no guest room available for them' (Luke 2:6–7). She and Joseph received this unexpected new life, the one promised to be the Saviour of the world, through a miracle. Mary must have felt not only awe and wonder over the gift of this child but the physical pain of giving birth along with her feelings of concern for this fragile young life. All from the humble surroundings of a stable.

Perhaps in those moments of delight and exhaustion she replayed with Joseph the visit of the angel Gabriel, who told her that she'd give birth to a son she was to name Jesus: 'He will be great and will be called the Son of the Most High. The Lord God will give him the throne of his father David, and he will reign over Jacob's descendants forever; his kingdom will never end' (Luke 1:32–33). What the angel said had happened – she had given birth to a son. But how he could be the Son of the Most High must have felt a mystery to his earthly parents.

This mystery manifests itself in Jesus as he turns the wisdom of the world on its head. He wasn't born in a palace but was placed into a manger, a feeding trough for animals. He ushered in his rule of peace and grace not through exhibiting power but through serving. And he became our Saviour through becoming a willing sacrifice, dying on an instrument of torture and rising to new life.

In the mess of our world, with the many contradictions we experience through moments of joy sometimes laced with sadness, I invite you to rejoice in the wonder of Jesus born to us. God in the form of a baby, there in Mary's arms.

Lord Jesus Christ, enlarge my understanding of the mystery of your birth, that I might rejoice in wonder and praise. Strengthen my faith in you as I face the paradoxes of rejoicing one moment and feeling sorrow the next. May your presence within me give me joy even in the difficult times. Amen

22

The angels shout, 'Glory!'

We arrive at church and take up a row, our parents bookending us, with me, the middle child, sitting in between my siblings. Having loosened our coats and removed our mittens and scarves, we wait for the Christmas service to start. After a few minutes, something unexpected happens. Instead of me counting down the minutes to the end of the service, meaning that we can go home to open presents, part of me cracks open in wonder and awe when we sing, 'O holy night'.[9] The words penetrate within me as I ponder it being the night of the dear Saviour's birth. I lose myself in the song – my soul feels the thrill of hope and I rejoice with the weary world. Not wanting to cause a commotion in church, much less endure the stare of my sister, I don't fall to my knees, but I do so in my heart as I worship the newborn Saviour.

Unexpected revelation. That's what I received that Christmas Eve many years ago, as did the shepherds even longer ago on the night of Jesus' birth. They didn't expect an angelic visitation as they kept the night watch, but out of the blue, the 'glory of the

Lord shone around them' when an angel of the Lord appeared (Luke 2:9). The angel told them not to be afraid, for 'I bring you good news that will cause great joy for all the people. Today in the town of David a Saviour has been born to you; he is the Messiah, the Lord. This will be a sign to you: you will find a baby wrapped in cloths and lying in a manger' (vv. 10–12).

The shepherds hardly had time to catch their breath or wonder about what this meant – a baby lying in a manger – when suddenly the whole sky filled with angels, 'a great company of the heavenly host', who praised God together: 'Glory to God in the highest heaven, and on earth peace to those on whom his favour rests' (vv. 13–14). They must have been overwhelmed by the glory.

Revelation in the ordinary. Glory in the everyday. We can't force God to reveal himself to us, but we can make ourselves open and available to receive his gifts of inspiration when they come. Why not spend some time today fostering an attitude of openness and receptivity to God's Spirit?

Holy God, you make yourself known in so many ways. In mystery; in the ordinary. Help me open myself up to your revelation, however you choose to show yourself to me during this Christmas season. May I humble myself before you and receive all that you have to give, that I might bring glory to you. Amen

23

Adoration of the shepherds

As we approach Christmas, I wonder if I've been naughty or nice. I'm mulling over an incident in which a neighbour had been caring for me and I got some instructions wrong, which made her fret. I turn her words of disappointment round and round, becoming increasingly anxious and distressed. I didn't mean to mess up. I didn't mean to make her worry. Will this careless act mean I won't have as many Christmas presents under the tree?

The thought lingers until finally Christmas arrives. My heart pounding, I glimpse the stack of presents under the tree, and as my parents pass them out, my pile increases and so does my joy. Through these tangible gifts, things that I'd hoped for and some wonderful surprises, I receive the greater gifts of grace, love and acceptance.

The shepherds received a surprising gift too. When the great angelic host appeared, they said to each other: 'Let's go to Bethlehem and see this thing that has happened, which the Lord has told us about' (Luke 2:15). They acted on the angels' revelation:

'So they hurried off and found Mary and Joseph, and the baby, who was lying in the manger. When they had seen him, they spread the word concerning what had been told them about this child, and all who heard it were amazed at what the shepherds said to them' (vv. 16–18).

As those on the lower rung of society, the shepherds may have felt they didn't deserve such an amazing gift. They could have mulled over the words spoken to them of being unworthy. But they obeyed the heavenly nudge and got to be the first visitors to see the baby Jesus. What they experienced so astounded them that they shared their story far and wide, and those who listened were also amazed.

Even though I fretted, my parents didn't hold back any presents that Christmas. I was overwhelmed by the sight and although I didn't realise it then, I shared with the shepherds the grace, surprise and joy of Christ's birth.

Do you love to give and receive presents? Like me, you might find them a fun way to express yourself when you have just the right gift for someone you adore. Or maybe you find them a challenge, as you fear you'll get things wrong and the person you love will be disappointed. Wherever you land, know that God showers you with his gifts each and every day. Spend some time pondering what he might want to give you and how you can open yourself to receive from him.

Loving God, you astound me with your goodness and your glory.
Instil in me wonder and surprise and help me to receive from you.
I may not feel deserving, but you accept me fully and want to
show me your love. Open my heart to all that you'd like to give.
Amen

24

Treasures of the heart

I hang up the phone with a smile, playing back the conversations with my American family. Because of the time difference, they are gathered round the tree opening their Christmas presents. Thousands of miles from them, I sit in front of my own tree, happy to have spoken with them. A few decades on from that first lonely Christmas in England, I'm now content with our Christmas traditions. I know I should go to bed – I arrived home some time ago from the midnight service and the kids will be up earlier than I want in their excitement for Christmas Day. But I relish the beauty of the lights as I ponder the gift of our Christmas Eve meal, the refrains of the carols and the sense of communion with family even separated by distance.

The gift of contemplating the wonder of the moment is one that Mary embraced: 'But Mary treasured up all these things and pondered them in her heart' (Luke 2:19). We're not told what scenes she played through in her mind, but perhaps along with considering what the shepherds shared she may have flashed back to the encounters over the previous months, such as meeting the angel Gabriel and visiting her cousin Elizabeth.

Although Mary questioned Gabriel about how the pregnancy would come about – with her being a virgin – she accepted the commission to be the mother of the Most High: 'I am the Lord's servant,' Mary answered. 'May your word to me be fulfilled' (Luke 1:38). Her humble obedience paved the way for God's redemptive plan of his Son being born a baby.

Then when she met Elizabeth, perhaps because she'd had more time to consider the gift of God choosing her, Mary cried out in song: 'My soul glorifies the Lord and my spirit rejoices in God my Saviour, for he has been mindful of the humble state of his servant. From now on all generations will call me blessed, for the Mighty One has done great things for me – holy is his name' (Luke 1:46–49). This wonderful song of praise, known as the Magnificat, resounds with her humble adoration of her God.

As you move through the Christmas season, don't miss out on the gift of taking a few moments to ponder the blessings and gifts you're enjoying. Even when we're experiencing sadness and loss, we can ask God to help us notice what he's bestowing on us. May we have eyes to see and a heart to receive all of what he wants to give.

Father of lights, you shine in the darkness. We worship and adore you; we praise your holy name. Thank you for the gift of life; thank you for hope and peace and love. Expand my sense of gratitude and give me strength for the things that I find difficult. May I share your love and life with others this Christmas season. Amen

25

Outsiders welcome!

On a whim, we invite him to our Christmas Eve feast. James is an older gentleman, one we know from the local community, and although he can be socially awkward, we look forward to welcoming him to our table.

The evening comes together with everyone entering into the conversation as it jumps from person to person, often with laughter as people share memories of Christmases past. At the end of the evening, as James takes his box of Christmas cookies, putting on his coat to leave, he turns to me and says, 'I wasn't sure what to expect tonight with this Christmas meal at the vicarage. It was surprisingly enjoyable – thank you for including me.'

'Outsiders' were warmly received at another celebration, the arrival of the God who became man. When they saw the rising star, the wise men recognised that the 'king of the Jews' had been born (Matthew 2:2). They travelled from the east to worship him, the first visitors from outside of the community, overjoyed to give the toddler

Jesus their treasures of gold, incense and myrrh. Jesus' mission to reach everyone in the world with his message of love, grace and forgiveness started at the beginning of his life.

We don't know how many of these wise men made this journey – the western church believes three did, because of the three gifts they brought, but the eastern church says there were twelve. The number doesn't really matter, though, for however many there were, they gave reverent honour to the King of kings. They did so having defied King Herod, who had instructed them to return and tell him where Jesus was. In ignoring his directions, they had to take the risk of Herod searching for them, capturing them and perhaps even killing them.

As we celebrate the season of Christmas, we can keep a focus on others with our festivities, perhaps inviting someone to join us for a special meal or a family gathering. At church we can look out for newcomers, welcoming them to our community. In our families, we can ask God to help us love the person with whom we might have some conflict.

As we worship Jesus, the one born to be King, may we bring to him our gifts and offerings as we receive his unwavering welcome.

Heavenly Father, I want to follow the example of the magi who came to worship your Son with adoration. Help me to persevere through hardship and trial as I seek your direction and as I receive your love and strength. I commit myself to serve you with love, joy and peace. Amen

Notes

1   See 'History of Christmas Trees', History.com, 27 October 2009 (updated 2 December 2020), **history.com/topics/christmas/history-of-christmas-trees**.

2   With insights from Ace Collins, 'Hark the herald angels sing', *Stories Behind the Best-Loved Songs at Christmas* (Zondervan, 2001), pp. 71–72.

3   See Erin Davis, *7 Feasts: Finding Christ in the sacred celebrations of the Old Testament* (Moody, 2020), p. 139.

4   In exploring Jesus as creator, I've drawn from the excellent little book by Bill Crowder, *Before Christmas: The story of Jesus* (Discovery House, 2019), pp. 79–97.

5   See, for instance, Hebrews 1:1–3 and Colossians 1:16–17.

6   See Andrea Skevington, *Jesus Said, 'I Am': Finding life in the everyday* (BRF, 2019), pp. 58–59.

7   I've been helped by the lovely little book by Ann Spangler, *Immanuel: Praying the names of God through the Christmas season* (Zondervan, 2007), pp. 126–129.

8   With insights from 'Gospel accounts of Mary and Joseph's journey gloss over the arduous reality of life and travel in ancient Galilee, scholars say', *LA Times*, 23 December 1995, **latimes.com/archives/la-xpm-1995-12-23-me-17102-story.html**.

9   Composed by Adolphe Adam with the English lyrics by John Sullivan Dwight.

About the author and artist

Amy Boucher Pye and **Leo Boucher** share their art and reflections from London and Minnesota.

Amy is an author, speaker and spiritual director. She's a regular contributor to several devotional publications, including *New Daylight* and *Our Daily Bread*, and her books include *7 Ways to Pray* and *The Living Cross*. She loves baking Christmas cookies and working out in body-combat classes.

Leo is a retired data-systems analyst and creator who paints in his art studio. He volunteers with his church and other organisations, including teaching art to seniors at retirement communities.

Find them at **amyboucherpye.com**.

How to use this book prayerfully – *visio divina*

A way of praying with art is known as *visio divina* – which is Latin for 'divine seeing'. It's simply a time of gazing at a painting and asking God to speak to us through it. You can engage with any of the paintings in this book through this practice. Here's how to do so, with the example of 'Mary treasuring all these things in her heart'.

1   Start with a prayer of invitation. As you welcome God to join you through his Spirit, ask him to calm you with his presence and help you to focus your mind and heart on him. You may wish to breathe deeply a few times to remind yourself how your physical being is connected to your inner being.

2   Gaze at the painting for a few moments, approaching it slowly. Notice what your eye focuses on, and spend a few moments there. Is it Mary? The angels? Jesus as a baby? What captures your attention?

3   As you interact with the images, ask God to speak to you. Might you sense a refrain from a song, a verse from Scripture, God's still, small voice? Don't strain for any of these ways God might speak to you but keep yourself open and ready to hear. For instance, God might touch your feelings or impress your thoughts with a new insight.

4   Respond to God through prayers of praise, intercession, adoration, petition, and so on. You may have moved away from the images in the painting, or not. Feel free to go where the Spirit leads.

5   Rest in God's presence, giving thanks for his love.

6   You could note in your journal, if you keep one, any insights you received or impressions you had during your time of prayer for consideration later.

Questions to spark prayer, reflection and discussion

Here are questions to use during Advent, either individually or with a group. You may prefer to engage with this book during the twelve days of Christmas.

Week 1

1 When you think of symbols of Christmas, what comes to mind?

2 I've heard it said that 'symbols bind up reality'. What does this mean? Why do you think symbols of Christmas are so potent and compelling?

3 Which Christmas carols give you the most joy and encouragement? Why?

4 How do you approach the culture's perception of Christmas? That is, how do you engage with such things as Father Christmas/Santa Claus, decorations, reindeer, Christmas crackers and others?

Week 2

1 What's been your experience of church? What has helped to heal and redeem any pain you've felt because of fellow Christians?

2 If you've experienced a 'blue Christmas', how has that shaped your Christmases afterwards?

3 What is your practice of gift-giving in the home? In the local community? Where you work or volunteer?

4 When you're feeling dark and gloomy, how do you foster a sense of light and life?

Week 3

1   Which of the six attributes of Jesus in this section – creator, human, light of the world, lamb of God, King of kings and morning star – resonates with you? Why?

2   In which gospel stories does Jesus' humanity shine through most for you?

3   How is Jesus similar or different to an earthly king? What does it mean for Jesus to be a king in your life?

4   'In Bible times people understood [the morning star] as signalling that the sun would soon rise' (p. 88). What signals in the world give you hope?

Week 4

1. Do you often travel at Christmas? Why or why not? If you do, how does that experience affect your celebration of the holiday?

2. If you were a witness in the stable, how might have you reacted to this baby? Why?

3. Why do you think God shared the news of his son's birth first to the shepherds?

4. As you picture the treasure box of your heart, what's there?

Enabling all ages to grow in faith

Anna Chaplaincy

Living Faith

Messy Church

Parenting for Faith

BRF is a Christian charity that resources individuals and churches. Our vision is to enable people of all ages to grow in faith and understanding of the Bible and to see more people equipped to exercise their gifts in leadership and ministry.

To find out more about our work, visit

brf.org.uk